D1457411

To:

_____

From:

_____

Give Mommy the Superglue

and Other Tips on Surviving Parenthood

John McPherson

Andrews McMeel
Publishing

Kansas City

Close to Home is syndicated internationally
by Universal Press Syndicate.

Give Mommy the Superglue
and other Tips on Surviving Parenthood

ISBN: 0-7407-1456-2
Library of Congress Catalog Card Number: 00-108481
www.uexpress.com
www.closetohome.com

"Okay, whichever name
the baby kicks at first
is the name we go with."

"Right now the baby is not
in the proper position for delivery,
but I'm confident it will shift
in time for your due date."

"Trust me on this. If we want the dog to bond with the baby right away, he needs to eat all of his meals off your stomach during the third trimester."

"The maternity nurse let me
borrow the other eight.
I just want to see the look
on my mother's face when she
walks through the door."

The latest in
greeting card technology:
audio birth announcements.

"That's it, little guy.
Get used to the feel of the handle.
Good, good."

"I worked out a deal with the woman in the apartment next door. She handles all of Jason's diaper changes for a buck a pop."

"So far five diaper services
have canceled us."

A hot new childcare product:
fortune diapers.

"He learned how to climb out,
so we greased the crib."

"Isn't that pop-up book
just the cutest thing?!"

Only a veteran mom
can master the art of
no-hands stroller opening.

"Mind?! Are you kidding?
Dad's gonna love being able
to get the mail while he's still
in his underwear!"

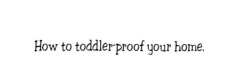

How to toddler-proof your home.

Having spotted some
acquaintances, Elaine activates
the Instant Grandchild Photo
Display in her purse.

"Will you just pick one! He's never going to recognize it."

"Okay, now. Give Mommy
the superglue."

"When I was a kid, we had to
get up, walk clear across
the room, and turn a dial
on the TV whenever we wanted
to change the channel!!"

At the National Sippy-Cup
Research Center